HOUSE

European Union Committee

8th Report of Session 2007–08

Current Developments in European Defence Policy

Report with Evidence

Ordered to be printed 26 February 2008 and published 7 March 2008

Published by the Authority of the House of Lords

London : The Stationery Office Limited

£8.50

HL Paper 59

The European Union Committee

The European Union Committee is appointed by the House of Lords "to consider European Union documents and other matters relating to the European Union". The Committee has seven Sub-Committees which are:

Economic and Financial Affairs, and International Trade (Sub-Committee A)
Internal Market (Sub-Committee B)
Foreign Affairs, Defence and Development Policy (Sub-Committee C)
Environment and Agriculture (Sub-Committee D)
Law and Institutions (Sub-Committee E)
Home Affairs (Sub-Committee F)
Social and Consumer Affairs (Sub-Committee G)

Our Membership

The Members of the European Union Committee are:

Lord Blackwell
Baroness Cohen of Pimlico
Lord Dykes
Lord Freeman
Lord Grenfell (Chairman)
Lord Harrison
Baroness Howarth of Breckland
Lord Jopling
Lord Kerr of Kinlochard
Lord Maclennan of Rogart

Lord Mance
Lord Plumb
Lord Powell of Bayswater
Lord Roper
Lord Sewel
Baroness Symons of Vernham Dean
Lord Tomlinson
Lord Wade of Chorlton
Lord Wright of Richmond

The Members of the Sub-Committee which carried out this inquiry (Foreign Affairs, Defence and Development Policy, Sub-Committee C) are:

Lord Anderson of Swansea
Lord Boyce
Lord Chidgey
Lord Crickhowell
Lord Hamilton of Epsom
Lord Hannay of Chiswick

Lord Jones
Lord Roper (Chairman)
Lord Selkirk of Douglas
Lord Swinfen
Baroness Symons of Vernham Dean
Lord Truscott

Information about the Committee

The reports and evidence of the Committee are published by and available from The Stationery Office. For information freely available on the web, our homepage is:
http://www.parliament.uk/parliamentary committees/lords eu select committee.cfm
There you will find many of our publications, along with press notices, details of membership and forthcoming meetings, and other information about the ongoing work of the Committee and its Sub-Committees, each of which has its own homepage.

General Information

General information about the House of Lords and its Committees, including guidance to witnesses, details of current inquiries and forthcoming meetings is on the internet at
http://www.parliament.uk/about lords/about lords.cfm

Contacts for the European Union Committee

Contact details for individual Sub-Committees are given on the website.
General correspondence should be addressed to the Clerk of the European Union Committee, Committee Office, House of Lords, London, SW1A OPW
The telephone number for general enquiries is 020 7219 5791.
The Committee's email address is euclords@parliament.uk

CONTENTS

Oral Evidence

Mr Andrew Mathewson, Director for Policy on International Organisations;
Professor Phil Sutton, Director, General Research and Technology;
Captain Richard Stokes, Assistant Director, Defence Equipment Plan, Ministry of
Defence

NOTE: In the text of the report:
(Q) refers to a question in oral evidence
(p) refers to a page of written evidence

Current Developments in European Defence Policy

REPORT

1. In this Report we make available, for the information of the House, the oral evidence given to the EU Sub-Committee C (Foreign Affairs, Defence and Development Policy) by Mr Andrew Mathewson, Director for Policy on International Organisations, Professor Phil Sutton, Director, General Research and Technology and Captain Richard Stokes, Assistant Director, Defence Equipment Plan, Ministry of Defence, on 29 November 2007; and correspondence from the Ministry of Defence.

2. Key topics in the evidence are:

   - Deployment and deployability of Battlegroups (QQ 3–8, 36, 53, 55–59, p 16);

   - The Nordic Battlegroup (QQ 8, 57, 58);

   - The UK's state of readiness (QQ 3, 12, 13);

   - Problems of force generation with particular reference to missions in Africa (QQ 5, 54, 55, 68, 69, 74, 75);

   - Availability of helicopters—in-house capability and the airlift market (QQ 9, 10, 59–62);

   - Availability of helicopters and the effects on aid delivery (QQ 43, 44, 49–52);

   - The Strategic Airlift Interim Solution Consortium and the C17 initiative (QQ 9, 58);

   - Purchase of A400M by EU Member States and pooling resources with EU partners (QQ 14–16, 29, 30, p 18);

   - The European Defence Agency (EDA) budget and different attitudes to spending (QQ 18, 23, 28, 29);

   - The EDA's role in the development of capability versus its role as an agent of industrial policy (QQ 24, 31–33);

   - The UK's attitude to Research and Technology (QQ 26, 27, 63–67);

   - The EDA's role in force protection (QQ 33–35, 38, 39);

   - Communications and information systems (QQ 37, 38);

   - Avoidance of duplication (QQ 45–48);

   - The extent of UK engagement in EDA projects (QQ 38–42, p 17);

   - Rapid reaction capability and matching force generation to political commitment (QQ 53–56, 69);

   - Medical facilities for missions (QQ 68, 70, 71, p 17);

   - The proposed EU police mission for Kosovo (QQ 71–73).

APPENDIX 1: SUB-COMMITTEE C (FOREIGN AFFAIRS, DEFENCE AND DEVELOPMENT POLICY)

The Members of the Sub-Committee which conducted this Inquiry were:

Lord Anderson of Swansea
Lord Boyce
Lord Chidgey
Lord Crickhowell
Lord Hamilton of Epsom
Lord Hannay of Chiswick
Lord Jones
Lord Roper (Chairman)
Lord Selkirk of Douglas
Lord Swinfen
Baroness Symons of Vernham Dean
Lord Truscott

Declaration of Interests

A full list of Members' interest can be found in the Register of Lords Interests:

http://www.publications.parliament.uk/pa/ld/ldreg.htm

APPENDIX 2: REPORTS

Recent Reports from the EU Select Committee

Evidence from the Ambassador of the Federal Republic of Germany on the German Presidency (10th Report, Session 2006–07, HL Paper 56)

The Commission's Annual Policy Strategy for 2008 (23rd Report, Session 2006–07, HL Paper 123)

Further Enlargement of the EU: Follow-up Report (24th Report, Session 2006–07, HL Paper 125)

Evidence from the Minister for Europe on the June European Union Council and the 2007 Inter–Governmental Conference (28th Report, Session 2006–07, HL Paper 142)

Evidence from the Ambassador of Portugal on the Priorities of the Portuguese Presidency (29th Report, session 2006–07, HL Paper 143)

The EU Reform Treaty: work in progress (35th Report, Session 2006–07, HL Paper 180)

Annual Report 2007 (36th Report, Session 2006–07, HL Paper 181)

Session 2007–2008 Reports prepared by Sub-Committee C

Current Developments in European Foreign Policy: the EU and Africa (4th Report, HL Paper 32)

Session 2006–2007 Reports prepared by Sub-Committee C

Current Developments in European Defence Policy (1st Report, HL Paper 17)

Current Developments in European Foreign Policy (16th Report, HL Paper 76)

The EU and the Middle East Peace Process (26th Report, HL Paper 132)

Current Developments in European Foreign Policy: Kosovo (32nd Report, HL Paper 154)

Current Developments in European Defence Policy (34th Report, HL Paper 161)

Current Developments in European Foreign Policy (38th Report, HL Paper 183)

Minutes of Evidence

TAKEN BEFORE THE SELECT COMMITTEE ON THE EUROPEAN UNION
(SUB-COMMITTEE C)

THURSDAY 29 NOVEMBER 2007

Present	Anderson of Swansea, L	Jones, L
	Boyce, L	Roper, L (Chairman)
	Chidgey, L	Selkirk of Douglas, L
	Crickhowell, L	Swinfen, L
	Hannay of Chiswick, L	Truscott, L

Examination of Witnesses

Witnesses: Mr Andrew Mathewson, Directorate for Policy on International Organisations, Professor Phil Sutton, Director General, Research and Technology and Captain Richard Stokes, Director, Defence Equipment Plan, Ministry of Defence, examined.

Q1 Chairman: Mr Mathewson, it is very good to be able to see you again today and we are very pleased also to meet your colleagues, Professor Sutton and Captain Stokes. As you know, we always like to see the Ministry of Defence after the meetings in Brussels concerned with the European Defence Agency and other defence matters, and I would be very grateful if your colleagues could introduce themselves for the record and then I will ask Admiral Boyce if he would ask the first question. Could you introduce yourselves first?

Mr Mathewson: Lord Chairman, thank you very much. It is, as ever, a pleasure to be here again. I am Andrew Mathewson; I am the Director of the Policy Team in the MOD that deals with international organisations. Before I pass the floor to my colleagues to introduce themselves can I just thank you for the questions which have been notified to us in advance? That was a great kindness and has helped us to make sure that we do have the right people here in order to, I hope, answer the questions you have posed to us. Secondly, may I just apologise that the letter we sent to you following the Steering Board arrived only fairly shortly before this meeting. The issue clearly was that the meeting in Brussels was only last week and you elected to have your examination of us slightly closer to the event than previously, which left us with a bit of a challenge in getting the letter out to you. So I apologise for the fact that you had it only shortly before this meeting.

Q2 Chairman: Could I say that in the light of that there is one question on the release of the extra €6 million which we will not be proceeding with because it was answered very fully in the Minister's letter.

Mr Mathewson: Thank you.

Professor Sutton: My Lord Chairman, my name is Phil Sutton and I am the Director General for Research and Technology in the Ministry of Defence and as such I have responsibilities for its research programme and, in particular, our relations with our international allies in collaboration on research.

Captain Stokes: My Lord Chairman, I am Captain Richard Stokes and I work in the area of the Equipment Capability Customer in an organisation called Director of the Equipment Plan. I am the military officer responsible for the ECC equipment capability contribution to the European Defence Agency.

Chairman: Thank you very much. Lord Boyce.

Q3 Lord Boyce: Next year we see the UK coming to the top of the EU's Battlegroup roster and I wonder if you would like to say whether you think we are going to be fully ready to deploy, given the fact that there are battalions across the Army which are currently under strength, and we know about the tempo of operations in Iraq and Afghanistan. So are we going to be ready to deploy at the drop of a hat or are we going to be nominally at the top of the roster and rather hope that we do not get caught out?

Mr Mathewson: The straightforward answer to that is yes, we will be ready to deploy. We have identified where the capability comes from and we will find our contribution to the Battlegroup from within the Joint Reaction Force, primarily focused on the capability within the JRF, known as the Small Scale Focus Intervention Battlegroup, which is one of the short notice standby capabilities within the JRF, and that battalion will provide the core of the capability and the enablers package will be assembled around it. So, yes, I think we will be ready; we have an exercise rehearsal programme which we have notified to the EUMS, which we have invited other Member States to come and witness. There is a final certification exercise in May. So, yes is the straightforward answer. The qualification I would make, though, is that clearly if there are other contingencies then we will have to judge those calls, and clearly we cannot rule out at the same time as we are the lead Battlegroup nation in the second part of 2008 that there would not be other national calls on the JRRF, and they would have to be judged alongside the Battlegroup. So, yes, we will be ready; but, yes we are aware of the fact of the risk of other calls on our forces. There is, of course, a second Battlegroup on the rota alongside us—it is a German-led Battlegroup in the second half of 2008, so the EU has an additional capability.

Q4 *Lord Boyce:* If I may, Lord Chairman, I think that we fully understand the contingency and of course the national call that may have to take priority if there is a conflicting demand at the same time, which could happen. Perhaps you would like to comment rather in the same way as in your answer to my first question, how is the process of making sure of the standby Battlegroup is ready, if you like? Does it go through the same process of preparation for that particular role in parallel with the lead Battlegroup, or is it rather static? Is it further back in notice terms should it be called upon because the lead Battlegroup gets taken away by a national or other priority?
Mr Mathewson: In fact there is no identification of one Battlegroup as lead and the other as standby; there are two Battlegroups which are both available at the same time and the Germans lead the other Battlegroup—the other Battlegroup, I should call it, rather than the second Battlegroup. It is a multinational Battlegroup with Germany, France and I think Belgium participating in it. They will be going through their own preparation certification and in principle the two Battlegroups should be at equal states of readiness from 1 July.
Chairman: Lord Hannay.

Q5 *Lord Hannay of Chiswick:* Could I follow up this question to get a slightly better and wider perspective of the EU Battlegroup performance? Has there ever been a deployment of an EU Battlegroup up to now, or has that never taken place? I cannot remember what exact status the deployment in the Democratic Republic of Congo was. Secondly, following on from that, does the Battlegroup mechanism enter into discussions when the EU undertakes a peace operations mission like the one in Chad or Central African Republic, or indeed in some aspects of the hybrid operation in Darfur? Is consideration given to

whether a Battlegroup could be inserted at the beginning of an operation in order to provide rapid deployment and then extract it when other troops who were not in the Battlegroup are made available, because it had always seemed to me, at any rate, that that was one of the purposes of having these Battlegroups? Though obviously it does not work if you cannot ever extract them once you have deployed them.
Mr Mathewson: In answer to your first question, there has been no Battlegroup deployment as such—and I say as such because I think elements of the German Battlegroup were raided at the time of the DRC deployment last year in order to generate some of the capacity for the DRC Mission. Also, the second Battlegroup was identified as the reserve for the DRC Mission last year. So there has been no formal deployment of the Battlegroup in accordance with its concept so far. Just to remind you that the concept reached full operational capability at the start of this year, so we are only within the first year of the concept. In answer to your second question, this is rather complex. Conceptually I think what you have outlined is entirely possible, that if the EU wanted to deploy rapidly it should look to its Battlegroup for a rapid ability to intervene and at the same time be generating the forces which are available for the follow-on force, so that the Battlegroup is not fixed in place because of a failure to generate forces. What we see in the case of the Chad Mission is very great difficulties in generating forces. We have had three-force generation conferences so far and there are still critical shortfalls in generating the forces required to do the mission which the EU thinks it should achieve. So conceptually one could have imagined if the EU wanted to respond quickly taking the decision to deploy the Battlegroup and then generating the forces for what comes next. The risk in that is that you do not identify the forces which come next and the Chad Mission has demonstrated the challenge that the EU still has and the problems that the EU has with generating what are, frankly, fairly modest sized forces—the EU is trying to generate a force of around 4000. Personally I think the risk is that the EU starts to look at the Battlegroup as almost its default force generation position and sees the Battlegroup as its first port of call when it is directing forces, whereas really it should be looking to the Battlegroup as its rapid response mechanism and calling on the forces which are, in theory, available through the force catalogue for longer term, more substantial missions.

Q6 *Lord Hannay of Chiswick:* Presumably you would agree that there is an equal risk that if the EU never uses the Battlegroups for rapid reaction

purposes they become an ornament on the wall rather than something that can be used.
Mr Mathewson: Yes.

Q7 *Lord Hannay of Chiswick:* I have no challenge with your saying that there is real risk if you used it all the time as the default option, but the other risk is as real, I would think.
Mr Mathewson: I think that is right; it is the "you must not use it in case you might need it" argument.

Q8 *Chairman:* Can I ask one supplementary to that? Is it possibly the case that countries have gone through the process of fielding a Battlegroup like, for example, the Nordic Battlegroup, which is going to be fielded in the first half of next year, and having gone through it they will retain some capabilities of deployability and therefore may be more ready to respond to subsequent force generation? Could the Battlegroup be seen in some ways as a training exercise or a transformation exercise for Member States?
Mr Mathewson: It is an exercise which I think raises the general level of deployable capability around the EU. The Nordic Battlegroup I think is an interesting case; in order to generate it they have done some investment in deployable equipment. To generate the people, though, they have taken, as I understand it, soldiers on special contract—this is the way Nordic countries generate their forces in that they contract for the forces specifically for that mission. So the personnel element of a capability will waste away when the contracted group of personnel run out of term on their contract. But the expertise, the understanding of how to do a deployable mission, the material investment will remain. So I would expect that in general the level of the Nordic countries' ability to do this sort of thing will have been raised by the experience of going through this.
Chairman: Lord Crickhowell.

Q9 *Lord Crickhowell:* That last answer just began to touch on the question that I wanted to ask as I still do not have a clear picture of these special groups. Up to now we have talked about forces and I immediately wrote down "lift capability". Only the other day in a rather different context Lord Malloch-Brown sat there and told us about the worldwide shortage of helicopters, and we had other evidence of that as far as our own forces are concerned. You used the phrase "deployable capability". Could you elaborate a little? Forces in terms of people, we know we are overstretched and we have touched on that; but if we did have the situation in a remote part where deployment is difficult, what is the general situation about the availability of the lift equipment and all the

other essential deployment equipment that would be needed to get the force there?
Mr Mathewson: If I look first of all at the British situation we have a range of strategic deployable capabilities, the C17s which are being bought, helicopters and sealift. We also use the market fairly extensively and I think we would have to assess the situation at the time: what are the demands on our in-house capability? To what extent can we use that? To what extent do we need to go to the airlift market, which we do very regularly now, so it would not be a novel departure? I think the way to see it would be that the in-house capability provides a base load and we go to the market for the peaks. So we would have to look at that and consider the extent to which we can use in-house capability or the extent to which we need to go to the market for either airlift or sealift for what is required on top of that. As to others, I cannot honestly speak for how each country is planning to meet its liabilities, but there are two initiatives to draw to your attention. One is the Strategic Airlift Interim Solution Consortium, which is a group of countries which includes the UK at the moment, which have bought in advance preferred access to some Ukrainian heavy lift aircraft, and there is an on-call contract, which a group of countries have participated in, partly through these liabilities. The second is the C17 initiative, which was announced at the Riga Summit, where a group of countries, including Sweden and I think Finland but others, have bought into a small number of C17s—I think five C17s—and they have bought a timeshare arrangement on those C17s. So these are ways in which countries are predicting their requirements. I guess also they would have to revert to the market, as we would.

Q10 *Lord Crickhowell:* You refer to the market and we have heard that there is a worldwide shortage of suitable helicopters in this other evidence that we have had. Do you think that the market is adequate around the world to provide for this sort of situation?
Mr Mathewson: There are different requirements. I think the market is adequate for the generic heavy lift. Also we are looking at options to provide helicopters to do normal freight lift within Afghanistan. The real shortage is in helicopters which are equipped with defensive aid suites, armour, night vision capability, the ability to do tactical operations, and that is where the shoe really pinches. But if you are looking at general freighting capability then there is much more capacity on the market for that; and certainly in Afghanistan we are looking at whether we can use the market to supplement what we have in-house to take on the freighting load to enable us to use our in-house capability for the tactical purpose.

Q11 *Chairman:* Could you perhaps confirm, Mr Mathewson, that those two initiatives, those cooperative initiatives are available both for NATO and for EU missions and therefore they have been designed for that purpose?

Mr Mathewson: Indeed, absolutely.

Chairman: Lord Swinfen.

Q12 *Lord Swinfen:* I think my questions have mainly been answered, but what is the UK Battlegroup purpose when it is not deployed on EU work? What is it doing and what has it just done? Has it just come back from Afghanistan or somewhere and so should be on a period of rest and training?

Mr Mathewson: I could write to you on the second question; I do not know what the unit has just done. One of the elements within the Joint Rapid Reaction Force will be one of the three battalion size units which are held at readiness for national contingencies. We normally have the spearhead lead element and an airborne group, which are within the Joint Reaction Force and available for short notice contingencies, and we would find the Battlegroup capability from within this standby capability which we hold in any event. But I could write to you on the question of what the units—which will be on the rota this time next year—will have done immediately before.

Q13 *Lord Swinfen:* It would be interesting because the services are haemorrhaging with fairly senior people but not with family upset.

Mr Mathewson: I think the qualification I would make is that in a sense they are on standby anyway for national requirements, that the requirement to be on standby for an EU purpose is not an additional burden placed upon them. They will be on standby because of a national requirement to be on standby because they are found from within the forces which we have on standby for national purposes. So they are not, as it were, additionally on standby for the EU.

Chairman: Lord Jones.

Q14 *Lord Jones:* On deployability it might be reasonable to ask you in terms of lift, the A400M has it flown yet? How many might we in Britain have and is Europe, the EU interested in purchasing that aircraft? Is it going to fly; are we going to have it; is it going to be important in terms of deployability?

Mr Mathewson: I do not think it has flown yet; we are going to have it. I cannot remember the numbers— Richard will tell you. A number of European countries are going to buy it; I cannot remember the numbers, but in considerable numbers. It will be important to us; it will replace an element of our C130 fleet and provide additional capability beyond what

that portion of the C130 fleet currently provides us. Richard.

Captain Stokes: My Lord, we are planning to buy 25 of the aircraft. I am not sure whether it has flown yet; I cannot answer that but I can certainly find out and let the Committee have a note. Other EU nations are procuring this; it is going to be the mainstay of the air transport fleet, certainly across Europe, for the foreseeable future. There is a proposal by France and Germany that they have submitted through the EDA to share basing and support of A400 aircraft. It is going to be interesting to see how that is taken up by some of the other nations because it will almost certainly offer benefits of scale, reductions in the cost of servicing and operating those aircraft, and I think it is an opportunity to which we should give time.

Q15 *Lord Swinfen:* It is not a paper aircraft, we are going to buy it and you assess it as being first rate and equal and superior to what is currently being used for lifting?

Captain Stokes: The C130s that we currently use are exceptionally capable aircraft—they are exceptionally capable aircraft—and the newest versions of those, although they have been in service in the US for some time, they are still relatively new to us. But over the life of the A400 it will offer us real benefits in the through-life cost of ownership I think, certainly.

Q16 *Lord Swinfen:* Are our own people looking forward to acquiring it and it is safe in terms of budget constraints that we read about and debate about?

Captain Stokes: I am not in a position to comment where we are in the planning round at the moment, my Lord.

Q17 *Chairman:* Perhaps I could ask one final on this question, you mentioned in your reply to Lord Boyce that there was going to be an exercise in May for the Battlegroup. I was wondering where that will take place and if it was not too far from London the Committee might ask if they could see it.

Mr Mathewson: I can tell you that it is called Exercise Druid's Dance but I cannot tell you where it is, my Lord.

Chairman: Lord Anderson with the next question.

Q18 *Lord Anderson of Swansea:* Before he retired on October 1 the outgoing Chief Executive, Nick Witney, wrote a valedictory dispatch of the long term vision in which he concluded as follows: "The EU is facing increased competition from Asia and the US while its competitiveness is declining. The upshot is that the EU's independence is at risk and its troops are not getting the most technically advanced equipment," and yet the UK appears to view its role in terms of the budget as totally minimalist as restraining others from doing things within the EDA. We recall, for example, that the former French Defence Minister, Michèle Alliot-Marie, called our attempt to reduce the budget last November a foolish one and put its position as a joke, she said, and again we sought to exempt ourselves from a series of initiatives in spite of that position in terms of the increased competitiveness. In an article in RUSI the former Director of Science and Technology at the MOD said that the relations between the UK and the EDA have "soured dramatically". This was written in June of this year. Why have relations soured so dramatically?

Mr Mathewson: I do not know that I would necessarily agree with that as a general characterisation. I think we have a difficult relationship with the EDA over the budget, but I think there are many areas of the relationship with the EDA on which we are able to work very closely and very supportively with them. So I would not accept that as a general characterisation, but I would accept that there are difficult aspects of our relationship and the budget is one of them. I think the background to this is our determination to get the best value for money from the investment we are able to make in capability.

Q19 *Lord Anderson of Swansea:* Is it candle end stuff? Have we lost what the former Executive called the long term vision of the challenge to Europe in terms of its competitiveness?

Mr Mathewson: It is certainly fair to say that the sums involved are relatively small, but the sums involved have to come from someone's budget in the Ministry of Defence, and if that requires a reduction in the capability within the MOD to acquire a certain level of capability then that explains our reluctance to, as it were, take a bit of a gamble on the EDA. I think there is, to be frank, a difference in vision of the EDA over the EDA between us and the French.

Q20 *Lord Anderson of Swansea:* We helped to write the remit.

Mr Mathewson: Yes, indeed.

Q21 *Lord Anderson of Swansea:* Including a very close link with ESDP.

Mr Mathewson: Yes, indeed.

Q22 *Lord Anderson of Swansea:* Have we gone back on that?

Mr Mathewson: No, I do not think we have. I think we are true to the remit. We see this as primarily an agency which identifies where countries can work together, which has a limited operational budget to

spend on studies, to help countries find where they can work together.

Q23 *Lord Anderson of Swansea:* Do we measure success by the extent to which we have reduced the budget?

Mr Mathewson: No, but I would fear that there are some on the other side who measure success by the extent to which they have been able to increase the budget.

Q24 *Lord Anderson of Swansea:* Is there a fundamental difference in perspective between ourselves and the French—as I have quoted the former French Defence Minister—in that they put the emphasis on armaments whereas we put the emphasis on capability?

Mr Mathewson: There is a difference. I think we see this as about developing capability. You do hear French Ministers—I certainly remember hearing Madame Alliot-Marie speak in terms of industrial policy. We do not see the EDA as an agent of industrial policy, but there are clearly some in France who have seen it in that way. There are clearly some in France who see the EDA as an aspect of building Europe and will speak about it in those terms and are prepared to invest in it as an aspect of building Europe at levels above which we think are justified by the capability development requirements of the agency. So we have, I think, an approach which is driven by value for money. The question for us is, is investing money through the agency going to help us develop a British capability? France has an approach which I think is more inclined to invest in Europe as an approach to developing the general level of European capability.

Q25 *Lord Anderson of Swansea:* And we are one of the big players—

Mr Mathewson: Indeed we are.

Q26 *Lord Anderson of Swansea:* ... in terms of investment in R & T and so on. To what extent are we isolated or do we bring with us a number of other participating countries?

Mr Mathewson: The current Chief Executive in recent commenting on the budget characterised it as 25 against one. I think he misleads his audience if he talks in those terms. There is a group of countries who have similar views to us.

Q27 *Lord Anderson of Swansea:* Nevertheless, as far as I am aware it has not been said of others that relations have soured, nor have the former Chief Executive and indeed the former Director of Science and Technology at the Ministry of Defence shown concern. Have those views expressed been elsewhere in respect of this minimalist position which we adopt? Are we basically on our own?

Mr Mathewson: My Lord, I do not think we are basically on our own. I think we attract particular attention because of our significance. We are the biggest investor in defence R & T in Europe, I think, and clearly because of the scale of our investment in defence capability and in defence R & T their frustrations with the UK, if such they are, assume a level of significance which they might not in respect of other countries.

Chairman: Lord Crickhowell and then Lord Hannay.

Q28 *Lord Crickhowell:* Can I follow up on this? We are in a rather surprising position in this Committee. Lord Tomlinson, who is no longer a Member, at most of our meetings would raise questions about whether the budgets were excessive and the lack of information about budgets. I must say that I am left a bit puzzled, having read the two letters from the Secretary of State, one dated 11 November and the latest of 26 November. I would find it helpful to get a clearer picture than I have of the general scale of the budget. Here we are objecting to what is proposed for the budget and we now know, following up the point that Lord Anderson made, that our position was not shared by all Member States. It would be nice to know exactly what that means. Therefore, discussions were only able to go on the budget for 2008 and the Secretary of State said that he negotiated an agreement of €20 million for the force functioning budget on the basis of only two new staff, not the six requested, and €6 million for the operational budget of which €1 million frozen, and so on. The incoming President, on the particular issue of controlled UAVs and so on, supported us, but I must say that compared with the normal numbers one hears in any defence context—indeed almost for any organisation—to a newcomer to this game who knows absolutely nothing about it these do seem the sort of tiny numbers which would get lost in almost any set of figures produced in any Ministry of Defence, or indeed almost any other departmental budget—they would disappear amid the decimal points. Can you give us a clearer picture of what is the overall cost and what we are getting for it and why we are making such a fuss about whether there are two or three more staff? This seems to me to be very unlike the normal approach to providing an effective defence operation. Explain, please.

Mr Mathewson: Gladly. There are two dimensions to this, I am afraid. The Agency normally tries to set a three-year financial framework, looking three years ahead, and that is the basis on which each year's annual budget is set. This year, as we did the last two years, we failed to set the three-year financial framework. I would say that the reason for that is the

Agency's inclusion in their projected budget over three years of this novel device of asking for €10 million for—the term is "earmarked funds", but they were unable to tell us what the funds were earmarked for. We and several other countries regarded this as an extension of the budget by stealth; that this device is supposed to be used only for a specific project, and we regarded it as rather improper to ask for money in the three-year framework for a particular project when in fact there was no particular project and it was a general contingency that they would expect to call on later. So we again failed to set the three-year financial framework and the Council of Ministers last week therefore again looked at setting the budget on an annual basis. There are three elements of the budget. The first element is the functioning budget, that which pays for its staff, its rent, its rates, its heat and light, and that was set at €20 million for the year 2008. Within that there was a discussion about how many additional staff the Agency required. The Agency asked for six additional staff; we saw no justification for increasing by six additional staff. We were eventually persuaded to compromise at two additional staff. I think there are those, as I mentioned earlier, who do see constant staff and budget growth as a measure of the Agency's vitality and we simply do not see that as a measure of the Agency's vitality. The second element of the budget is the operational budget, i.e. that element of the budget which is available to the Agency to spend on studies, technical examinations and the like. We agreed that that budget would be €5 million with the option of a further one million justified at the midpoint of the year. I agree with you small sums, but these are all small sums which have to come from someone's budget in the MOD and they are small sums which would not be available to that person to spend on capability through another route in the MOD. So there are always opportunity costs, even for small sums. The third element of the budget this year was this novel introduction of using earmarked funds and they asked us for €8 million next year for a project to examine the EDA's role in inserting UAVs—Unmanned Aerial Vehicles—into controlled airspace, and we regard this as a very serious priority indeed; it will be a real step forward if we can have UAVs flying in controlled airspace. We are not yet clear what the Agency's role in that might be; we think it is more likely to be in the area of certification, standards, regulation than in the area of technical examination, and we agreed to allow them to plan on €6 million for that if they come to us during the course of the year with a convincing business case as to why the Agency can spend this money wisely. The overall point is that these are small sums of money but these are small sums of money, all of which have an opportunity cost and the Agency needs to work

with us to identify how it can add value to what we are doing because that is the way to persuade us to invest, rather than running the argument that this is about building European capability or building Europe.
Chairman: Lord Hannay.

Q29 *Lord Hannay of Chiswick:* Firstly, could I follow up the budgetary implications of what I think Captain Stokes said was a Franco-German initiative with regard to the A400M, which they had suggested led to some EDA activity. You did not say what our reaction was likely to be to this proposal and it would be interesting to know whether we think it is something we would wish, since we are going to be a purchaser of A400Ms, to participate in. Secondly, would that then mean a substantial increase in the EDA budget or would it be done entirely on the basis of national buy-in to the cooperation? So that is the first question. The second question is the matter of budgetary technique, which has come home to me with considerable pain when I heard it being explained because most of my life dealing with the EU was dogged by Her Majesty's Treasury's insistence that 18% of every penny that was spent in Brussels had to be docked from somebody's budget here. No doubt the percentage figure has changed as the European Union has got bigger but the principle has not. This is one way of looking at budgeting and control of public expenditure, but it does become uniquely damaging to us when it turns out that 26 other Member States do not do the same thing: that is to say, could you tell us does the French government insist that every penny spent by the EDA has a percentage of it docked from the French defence budget? Does the German, Italian, Romanian—I do not mind who it is? But if the answer is, as I suspect it is, that they do not then you have an answer to your problem as to why we have a difference in approach. We have it built-in not at the demand of the Ministry of Defence but at the demand of Her Majesty's Treasury, who certainly have not abandoned an interesting candle end since Mr Gladstone was there.
Mr Mathewson: Shall I take that question whilst Captain Stokes gathers his thoughts on A400s? No, I am afraid you have not accurately captured the position there, my Lord. The contribution to the EDA budget comes from the Ministry of Defence and the consideration is simply whether it is good value for money in terms of MOD budget holders to invest in the EDA rather than spending that money in developing capability down another route. So it is a question of affordability and opportunity costs within the MOD. There is no real engagement with the Treasury in the terms which you have described. My understanding is—and I think in answer to a question from this Committee about a year ago we

did a call around other MODs and we basically funded the same way—all participating Member States are essentially funded from the general defence budget and are all, therefore, considering their own value for money considerations. But I think in some cases those value for money considerations are overlaid by the issues of the principle of building European capability, and I think that is the issue that separates us and France rather than the one you described, my Lord.
Chairman: Lord Boyce.
Lord Boyce: This is a follow-on. If the MOD budget is stretched across the board then clearly Lord Hannay's point is especially relevant. If the Treasury is not going to allow room for the defence budget to meet its own programme then the EDA is likely to be the first casualty in any savings exercise.

Q30 *Chairman:* I am sorry, Captain Stokes, you were not given the chance to answer. This topic of this idea of pooling in this sort of way is something which we have been interested in before and indeed one of our colleagues, not on the Committee, the late Lord Gardiner, always took a particular interest in this as a way forward.
Captain Stokes: The French-German initiative is broadly aimed at those smaller nations who might perhaps want to buy a smaller number of A400s for which it would not make sense for them to procure their own support and training infrastructure. The UK approach at the moment to A400s on the basis of investment appraisal is that it is more cost effective to deliver the through-life support in the UK, although we are aware of the French-German proposal. One area that we are also considering away from the support area is in training and we are considering the possibility of sharing simulator facilities with France, possibly either in France or the UK. So the whole principle of sharing support services or training facilities where it is cost effective to do so is something that is very much considered as part of the procurement process. A good example of where we are doing something fairly similar is in our procurement of C17s, the fifth and possibly the sixth C17, where there is another initiative, the strategic airlift capability, a NATO-EDA initiative to look at sharing a number of C17s with other European nations, and we are considering the possibility of using the UK facilities at Brize Norton as a means of supporting those additional aircraft where it is cost effective to do so.
Chairman: Lord Truscott.

Q31 *Lord Truscott:* Just to focus on capabilities are you satisfied with the progress achieved since the last Steering Board meeting in the area of capabilities development? Particularly bearing in mind that the

MOD is regarded as focusing on the need to develop capabilities rather than EU institutions. I notice that the Secretary of State refers to that in his letter of 26 November, where he says that the long term strategy and objectives will add value to European capabilities, and is this perhaps where some of the strain is between the UK focusing on the capabilities and some other EU Member States focusing on long term objectives, strategies and institution building?
Captain Stokes: The strand of work that I have been most closely involved with is the whole area of capability planning. When the Agency was first started there was little in the way of a structured approach to capability planning and over the last 18 months a substantial amount of work has been done, led by the Agency but strongly supported by the UK in developing their capability development plan. This takes work from the headline goal 2010 exercise in identifying the relatively near term European capability shortfalls. It also identifies the long term shortfalls and long term priorities, looking out to 2020, and we have used a lot of UK resources to support that development work and we are getting to the stage now where we have a much, much clearer picture of the longer term shortfalls, the longer term requirements to meet the headline goal requirements. So in terms of process we have done a lot with them. How are we involved? The UK is involved in about one-third of the EDA project teams. We have very clear criteria about those that we wish to be involved with. In the key areas of shortfall that have been previously identified, force protection, the probability and information superiority, we are moving on much further than originally anticipated. Deployability we have already spoken about at some length but I can talk about force protection and information superiority.

Q32 Lord Truscott: It is a point though that it still seems to be focusing on the process rather than the actual development of the capabilities themselves.
Captain Stokes: I think we are taking both strands in parallel. There needs to be a long term process to identify where the effort should be focused and without that process the opportunity was just focused on individuals and specific items that did not fall into the strategy. So I think the approach the Agency has taken and we have supported is absolutely the right one—we take both strands as of equal importance.
Chairman: Lord Jones.

Q33 Lord Jones: What action is being taken by us as a government and in Europe to address the three critical capability shortfalls in force protection, deployability and information superiority?

Mr Mathewson: Can I ask Captain Stokes to take that question, but if I may may I add a little in response to Lord Hannay? I think there is a point which Lord Hannay raised which Captain Stokes did not properly answer. It was the question that if there is a cooperative approach agreed to support within the European Defence Agency supporting A400s, would that money come from the Agency itself or from national budgets? The answer is that it would come from national budgets and I think the answer to Lord Truscott's question about why is progress so slow actually comes down to national budgets as well. The Agency's role is to find the areas where the nations want to come together and spend their money. If their money is tight and they are not prepared to invest in these capabilities then the Agency can only lead the horse to water.

Q34 Lord Jones: Question 5 formally!
Captain Stokes: I can talk about the UK's position and how we have moved forward in those areas, and also the work that the European Defence Agency is doing in each of those capability areas, but I cannot really speak about the progress each individual EU nation is making in those areas. Taking the first one, force protection, the UK has done a lot of work obviously to support current operations in the area of force protection. A lot of that which has been done over the last four years has been through urgent operational requirements. You will be aware that some £2.3 billion from the Conflict Prevention Fund has been spent on urgent operational requirements and around 60% of that is on force protection of all kinds, both individual force protection, collective force protection in the air, the land and the sea environments. That is supported by a long term programme for force protection across all of the environments and the Research and Technology Programme which supports it as well. So there are comprehensive programmes there. Then just a few examples of those—patrol vehicles, Osprey and Kestrel, body armour, infrared cameras for aircraft and a very large number of classified programmes to protect individuals on operations currently in Iraq and Afghanistan. The European Defence Agency has also commissioned a major research programme into force protection, in which 20 of the 26 Member States are participating. The UK made a judgment not to participate in that particular programme and the principal reason for that is because of the amount of work that we are already doing nationally and we consider ourselves very much at the leading edge of a lot of the force protection work. We are keeping a watching eye on that work, however, and subject to security constraints we will be prepared to share some of our experiences with the Agency as their work goes forward.

Q35 *Lord Jones:* In terms of sharing, do you have confidence now that we are a bigger outfit in Europe that you can share?

Captain Stokes: Force protection is a particularly problematic area because of security constraints, but as a matter of principle, sharing our experience is something we would be willing to do with the Agency.

Q36 *Chairman:* Various people have supplementaries but are you going to say something about deployability and information superiority?

Captain Stokes: I could talk about deployability. We have mentioned already the 25 A400 aircraft. The other area where we have moved forward substantially is on rotary wing helicopter lift, in particular the announcement to convert the eight Mark 3 Chinook aircraft to operational standard but also the purpose of six Danish Merlin helicopters is about to make a substantial improvement in our availability of medium and heavy lift helicopters. On information superiority, again a large amount of work in progress; it is a massive area that covers everything from intelligence collection and surveillance all the way through to processing and dissemination of that information and sharing it at the tactical, operational and strategic levels. One particularly important issue for us is our policy requirement to be able to lead an operation, either in an EU Battlegroup or in a NATO context, and ensuring that we place sufficient priority on having the ability to communicate interoperability between participating nations, which is something that we are currently addressing.

Q37 *Chairman:* With respect to Captain Stokes, could you just say something about what the EDA has done in that area?

Captain Stokes: The EDA has a number of project teams working in the information superiority area, of which we belong to seven or eight of them, looking at communications and information systems, information exchange requirements, which is not just about technology but is also about process and procedures as well, and making some large improvements there. Satellite communications, network enabled capability, we have made some substantial contributions into a major EDA study into what NEC means across the participating nations. And the final one is radio spectrum and frequency management.

Q38 *Chairman:* Are most of these projects being participated in by the majority of EDA members?

Captain Stokes: I cannot give you the exact numbers, my Lord, but the majority have at least eight to ten members and some substantially more.

Chairman: Lord Anderson.

Lord Anderson of Swansea: Before I come to helicopters, you mentioned, I think, that we are disengaging from force protection. From how many other EDA initiatives have we in the UK disengaged?

Chairman: Not engaged; we were never in it.

Q39 *Lord Anderson of Swansea:* Not engaged is probably better than disengaged, yes.

Captain Stokes: If we look at it from the number of project teams that are commissioned we are involved with about one-third of the project teams. The different project teams are very much at different stages—some are in very, very early conceptual work and some of them much later. But we make a very conscious decision to look at the potential benefits to the UK of each of these project teams, both in terms of potential projects and in terms of what we can contribute.

Q40 *Lord Anderson of Swansea:* Can you give us some comparative data on other countries and the extent to which they have not engaged in such initiatives, particularly France, for example?

Captain Stokes: I am sorry; I do not have that information.

Q41 *Lord Anderson of Swansea:* No, if you could give us a note on this. You say that we are participating in perhaps one-third and I wonder whether that is part of the reason why relations are said to be soured between ourselves and the EDA because we are semi-detached.

Captain Stokes: We can let you have a note.

Q42 *Chairman:* Just on this particular point, if we could just pursue this. You talk about these projects being in different stages of development. Is it a question you either join at the start or you do not join, or is it possible that perhaps a project which we might have been sceptical about at the start, after a period of time does appear to be more promising, and can we have a chance to join later?

Captain Stokes: My Lord, the nature of the project teams is very different between each of the teams. We can join at any stage and we can leave at any stage. But they are not the same as a traditional UK project team that is there to manage the concept assessment, demonstration of bringing introduction to service. The general principle we have in a project team is to bring interested groups of nations to see if they can identify shared requirements, common requirements in a common time scale. So usually you can see fairly early on whether it is something in which you might have an interest in that capability area in the same time scale as an international requirement.

Q43 *Lord Anderson of Swansea:* When we talked about heavy lift, I think it was Lord Crickhowell who raised the point, you gave a very full reply in respect of not only the revamped Hercules but the Ukrainian Antonovs and so on. When we did have Lord Malloch-Brown before us he mentioned particular shortfalls in respect of helicopters, saying we were scrambling around to find groups of helicopters available for Darfur and other key areas. What is the position of the EDA in respect of pooling research on helicopter development?

Mr Mathewson: While Captain Stokes is gathering his thoughts, we through NATO identified a process of trying to examine why there are so few helicopters available for operation in grounds like Afghanistan, against the background that when forces are declared to NATO there seem to be far more helicopters in theory available. So what are the reasons why the helicopters which are in theory in the catalogue are not being provided? There are a variety of reasons which nations have identified—some to do with training, some to do with a particular mark of a helicopter, some to do with its ability to operate at high altitude and in hot climates, and some to do with defensive aid suites. What we have been encouraging both through NATO and the European Union is for countries to try to come together where they have a similar issue, and we have asked to be inserted into the EDA's work programme for next year some work in this area. Are there groups of countries which have a similar helicopter, which faces a similar challenge in adapting it to the modern environment? For example, we understand that there are a number of countries which have substantial numbers of former Soviet helicopters—can we encourage them through the Agency, therefore, to come together to work out how they might equip these for the current operational environment? This is not the high tech, the leading end of science, it will often be fairly basic adaptations, and it does, I have to say, require those countries to want to spend the money to do it.

Q44 *Lord Anderson of Swansea:* Could there be a leasing capability possibility? I believe when the Germans certainly initially went to Afghanistan they were leasing Antonovs from the Ukraine—that is on the heavy lift, particularly on the helicopters now.

Mr Mathewson: There are options and, as I think I mentioned earlier, in Afghanistan NATO has decided to let a contract for some of the basic helicopter roles, some of them just carrying freight around, so that the helicopters that have more specialist requirements are available for the more specialist roles. So there are certainly levels of capability required and in some cases you can lease the capability and that is what NATO is trying to do south of Afghanistan, hire in a capability just to do

the logistical supply role in a fairly unthreatening environment, which allows the helicopters, which are available with more specialist capability to be used on the more demanding roles.

Q45 *Lord Anderson of Swansea:* Is the EDA also involved in this in seeking to identify areas where leasing can solve the immediate problem?

Mr Mathewson: This issue is on their work plan. It will depend to a very large extent on how countries want to respond. This often comes back to whether there are countries that want to solve the problem and want to use the EDA to solve the problem.

Q46 *Chairman:* But if it is on NATO's work plan that it is doing it we presumably have to be careful not to duplicate it and do the same thing twice with largely the same people, and there clearly should be some sensible division of labour on some of these things, presumably? Should be?

Mr Mathewson: My concern is not that there are too many people getting into the business of upgrading helicopters but that there are too few people getting into the business of upgrading helicopters.

Chairman: My Lord Swinfen has been trying to get in on this for some time.

Q47 *Lord Swinfen:* You were saying that other people are looking at force protection and that we are not working with them at the moment, but they will also be learning the lessons, albeit second hand, from Afghanistan and Iraq. What is being done to make certain that there is no duplication? Do I gather from that that nothing is being done?

Professor Sutton: We have a close liaison with various of the technology groups associated with these programmes and therefore, as Captain Stokes explained, we are perpetually in a position where we are able to observe and be part of, so we do keep close with those programmes. At this stage we have not seen anything significant coming through at all that suggests that there is any real advantage that that work is offered to date. But you are exactly right; we do need to keep in contact with that.

Q48 *Lord Swinfen:* You are happy for another country to pay for the work rather than ourselves?

Professor Sutton: It s not so much that, my Lord, it is a question of we are a long way ahead of the field at the present time and we do not expect at this stage to be able to see anything, sadly, that would give us that advantage. But we remain hopeful.

Chairman: Lord Crickhowell.

Q49 *Lord Crickhowell:* Earlier all of the witnesses, understandably, were anxious to protect the Ministry of Defence's budget but as Lord Malloch-Brown made absolutely clear in his evidence to this Committee, when talking about aid, said this is an issue that goes far beyond the Ministry of Defence. He spoke of a worldwide shortage of helicopters making it impossible for some of the aid work to be effectively carried out. He actually pressed us, rather surprisingly, to ask some questions about the whole issue, and he was obviously anxious for information. I wonder how much of the work that you are doing in making enquiries about the worldwide market and all these connected issues is being closely coordinated jointly with the other departments that must have an interest? Surely this is an area where we really should have joined-up government and it is not simply a defence matter? Clearly we do need to have a picture right across government of the worldwide market and its availability and the way in which the various departments of government who require helicopters can get into that market effectively. Are you, is the Ministry of Defence working with other departments or is there more scope than is being exercised at present for doing so?

Mr Mathewson: I am not entirely sure that we have seen the analysis that says there is a worldwide shortage of helicopters. We have certainly seen the analysis that says there are not enough helicopters equipped for the roles which we want our Armed Forces to be able to undertake; but I think there are additional helicopters which are not so specially equipped which are available. So at the moment I am not sure we recognise an analysis that there is a worldwide shortage of helicopters—there are scarce capabilities.

Lord Crickhowell: This Committee is not just the defence Committee for the European Union; it also covers the other topics, such as aid. I must say I think we would be quite interested to discover more about this general picture, wider than the Ministry of Defence. Anyway, I leave the thought, if I may, with you, whether this is a question that goes wider than simply the Ministry of Defence as it seems to me a pity if there is no wider investigation of it going on within government.

Chairman: We will be returning to this question on the last question which we have this morning, which really does respond to the points.

Lord Crickhowell: It would be helpful to have a paper on this.

Chairman: I would like us to protect the last question.

Q50 Lord Hannay of Chiswick: I have a follow-up. You said that you were not aware of the situation. My recollection is that there was a really serious problem in helicopter lift in the case of the Pakistan earthquake of 18 months ago, which was not a military problem at all because nobody was suggesting conducting military operations in Azad

Kashmir—it was a simple problem that they could not find around the world enough people ready to deploy the helicopters in time, but perhaps my memory is faulty.

Mr Mathewson: Again, I have not seen the analysis that points to a worldwide shortage. There is within NATO an analysis of why when there are on the face of it plenty of helicopters available within national Armed Forces there are so few available in Afghanistan.

Q51 Lord Hannay of Chiswick: I would regard that as much the same thing, to be honest with you.

Mr Mathewson: I think it has come down to largely the specialist capabilities which we require in Afghanistan rather than the raw numbers of helicopters themselves.

Q52 Chairman: There is presumably, Mr Mathewson, a difference between the absolute number of helicopters and the readiness of Member States to deploy them for particular functions?

Mr Mathewson: I think the readiness is certainly in issue and helicopters which are required in Afghanistan have to fly at high altitude and in hot climates, and in many cases to have armour and in many cases to have other defensive aid suites. In some cases the crews will require specialist training, and our analysis is that these issues are more crucial for the Afghanistan problem than simply the shortage of air frames, that it is the specialism that is required rather than the simple shortage of air frames.

Chairman: Lord Boyce.

Q53 Lord Boyce: On 19 November the High Representative Javier Solana talked about development in the area of rapid reaction and the future development of an EU rapid reaction concept. I would like you to expand on that slightly and say what is the EU's aspiration to have an ability to take very rapid reaction in the event of a crisis. I would be particularly interested if you could explain something of the political process which would allow action, (albeit the Battlegroup or whatever being ready to go), the grindingly slow process that normally happens in trying to get Member States to agree and the chain of command above the military command into the PSC or whatever.

Mr Mathewson: The starting point for this is the Battlegroups, which we touched on earlier. There is a roster of Battlegroups available at short notice. I think the requirements are to have the first elements on the ground within five days and to be fully operational within ten days of the political decision to go. I will check those numbers but there are defined criteria for what rapid response means in the case of the Battlegroup. The EU Military Committee is additionally looking at the requirements for maritime and air rapid response. We do not think that that requires a standby force in the same way as is required for land forces—that maritime forces and air forces are inherently more rapidly deployable. But we think that the EU does need a mechanism for identifying those forces which nations have, which are at the shortest rates of readiness and being able to identify what capability is available for them to plan on and to draw forward forces which are at shorter periods of readiness. The work on the air and maritime rapid response capability is going on now and they will sit alongside the land capability, which is essentially the Battlegroups, and there will be discussions about the mandate for doing work on the overall rapid response capability. But I think you are absolutely correct to identify the political problem as much as the military problem. It is one thing to be able to have the forces available to deploy within a period of a decision but what we have found is that it is the period leading up to the decision which is where the delay really comes in.

Q54 Lord Boyce: My question is whether any effort has been made to streamline that process? For example, allowing a reconnaissance party to depart before the order to depart is given. But also whether anybody has made a conscious effort to try and streamline the process, which is turgid, to put it mildly.

Mr Mathewson: The EU military staff have fairly well developed procedures for identifying what the options in a military response might be, for conducting a recce. There has been a recce into Chad which shaped the formation of the options which were then put to the PSC. It is difficult, though, to see how you can accelerate political considerations simply on the basis of improved process. This does come down to political willingness to get involved in the operation and the political appetite for the particular operation in question at the time. That is largely the issue over the Chad Mission—it is the different countries' willingness to be involved in the Chad Mission rather than the readiness at which their forces are held. This will often come down to simple political considerations of their appetite for that mission.

Q55 Lord Boyce: Can you remind us whether or not the decision to deploy the Battlegroup is qualified or is unanimous in terms of voting, and if a country has an element in a Battlegroup and it decides that it does not want to support the Battlegroup's deployment can it extract its elements so that the Battlegroup can actually move ahead?

Mr Mathewson: The decision to deploy any EU military mission will be by unanimous decision. Clearly that leaves countries open the option to support the decision but without being willing to participate in it, and that is the position which we are in over Chad. We support the EU's willingness to deploy a mission with Chad, albeit that we have made clear that we will not have forces to contribute to the mission. In principle, if a country has committed to a Battlegroup then its forces, which form part of that Battlegroup, ought to deploy with the Battlegroup. But clearly you can never rule out either that the nation considers that its forces are unsuitable for the particular mission that is envisaged or that it has other contingencies running at the time, or that it simply does not want to participate in that mission for whichever political reason. So, yes, countries could in theory withdraw their forces from a Battlegroup. The impact of that on the Battlegroup will, I think, vary from case to case. There are clearly cases where nations have contributed niche capabilities to a Battlegroup which are not critical to the Battlegroup going, and which the framework nation might be able to replace from its own resources at the time. Clearly in other cases the contribution would be more.

Q56 Lord Boyce: It is reasonable to presume that it is the case that the idea of having a very rapid reaction force is not likely ever to materialise?

Mr Mathewson: I think it is fair to say that the further you get from a Battlegroup which is provided by one nation the more complications there are.

Q57 Chairman: On the other hand, having had some discussions with the Swedes, who are the lead country in the Nordic Battlegroup, they have obviously been working very hard to try and make sure that they can fit together and certainly a multination Battlegroup seems to be rather impressive.

Mr Mathewson: I think what the Swedes have done is very impressive and we have best visibility of what the Swedes of done and less visibility of what other Battlegroups have done. And they have practised at the political level as well as the military level. They have had exercises involving their ministers and political decision-making. I think the Swedish approach to this is exemplary; we have less visibility of what others might have done in the same area.
Chairman: Lord Swinfen.

Q58 Lord Swinfen: Is the lift capability also on standby or when there is a crisis do we have to look around, find aircraft and hire them?

Mr Mathewson: Countries will have to look around and find aircraft from whichever source. The Swedes have clearly participated in the C17 consortium and are clearly assuming that their purchase into the C17 consortium will be available if they have to deploy their Battlegroup.

Q59 *Lord Swinfen:* We have a Battlegroup that is going to be available in January, I believe. Do we have designated aircraft?
Mr Mathewson: No.

Q60 *Lord Swinfen:* Where are we going to get them?
Mr Mathewson: We will have to look at the situation at the time; we will have to see whether the situation requires airlift or sealift.

Q61 *Lord Swinfen:* I am assuming at the moment it is airlift. In most places we would have to go it would be quicker to move them by air.
Mr Mathewson: If the situation requires truly rapid response. I think it is the same answer as I gave earlier, that we have in-house capability; we will have to assess the availability at the time alongside whatever else is going on.

Q62 *Lord Swinfen:* All the RAF transport aircraft are servicing in Iraq and Afghanistan at the moment.
Mr Mathewson: So we will have to look at options like the strategic airlift interim solution, which we are contracted into, or use of the market. As I said earlier, use of the market is not novel; this is not a controversial part of our logistics plan. The in-house capability provides the base level of capability and we routinely—virtually daily—go to the market to provide for peak loads. I think we would see this as one of those peak loads.
Chairman: Lord Crickhowell.

Q63 *Lord Crickhowell:* Can we move on to R & T? How will the Strategy on Defence R & T, adopted at the Steering Board Meeting, help the EU—and I quote Dr Solana—"spend more, spend better and spend more together"?
Professor Sutton: First of all, my Lord, it was not the strategy that was supported by the Board but a framework document which actually set down the criteria for how such a strategy would be put together. The Board also charged the Agency with getting its research and technology directors from the Member nations together and to develop that strategy on some form of an agreed approach. So that is really the next step in this action. I am very pleased to say, however, that the UK is already leading a group looking at where there might be opportunities for a common interest and so forth, so we are trying to be in a good state for when that strategy is put together. But there is no time table yet for when the R & T Directors will meet, although in fact I have had a discussion with the current Chief Executive,

Alexander Weis, who is planning to get that group together in the spring. He has not given a date yet but that is his intention.

Q64 *Lord Crickhowell:* This is an area which the Secretary of State has endorsed—he has endorsed the framework for the purpose of his letter. Reading the document it is a fairly lengthy statement of what is envisaged and what might be the advantages to various groups—national governments, industry and so on. As we are endorsing it I would like you to comment a little further on what we see the advantages are for this country. Clearly one's instincts are right that it must be a good thing to identify what are common priorities and who is working on them and who is ready with what and when, and the other points dealt with in the framework document. Could you elaborate a little more because it may enable us to judge better the value of the whole exercise?
Professor Sutton: Gladly. I should again restate that we are always driven in our thinking, including for research and technology, on meeting our military capability needs—that is always what is behind our thinking. As such we prepared and released a Defence Technology Strategy very recently which very much embodied the UK's view and the Ministry of Defence's view about how various areas of technology would enable it to move towards meeting our future capability needs. So we would hope in working with our colleagues across Europe that we would be able to get them to think in terms also of how their research efforts would similarly look towards meeting capability needs. The key part, of course, is seeing where those capability needs align and one must be careful in that one might be able to agree a fairly high level topic but depending upon how one is going to deliver that in capability terms it may be that there is a subtle or perhaps quite important variation between various Member States. So looking for Members who have common areas of interest and certainly from our perspective based on a capability driven need.

Q65 *Lord Crickhowell:* I do not see any reference, from a very quick read, to the academic world, to the university world. I am not quite clear into which the main efforts are to be directed. Clearly there are international manufacturing concerns doing their own research and development as part of the development of products and so on, but this is an area presumably which extends far beyond the efforts of individual companies or the individual national government research efforts. Is it part of the framework to bring the university and the academic world into this exercise?

Professor Sutton: I believe it is expected that the Member nations will make sure that the connections exist between their respective industries and academia and so forth, and indeed from the UK's perspective looking to our own indigenous defence research programme that is very much at the heart of what we are trying to achieve. And following on from the Defence Industrial Strategy we are looking for good and effective ways to work with our industry; we are looking to work with the research councils that of course fund universities and so forth—a rich seam of possibilities, something like £2.8 billion a year, I believe. So that would be the conduit I would suggest for how this would happen.

Q66 Chairman: But is there a problem in this given the considerable range between the sort of R & T expenditure in which the UK engages and the R & T expenditure which presumably the majority of Members of the EDA engage in, which is obviously a relatively small fraction of what we do. How many problems arise because of this spectrum?

Professor Sutton: Certainly, as you correctly say, Lord Chairman, the difference in spending between various Member States is quite significant, with the UK and France being the largest contributors by far.

Q67 Lord Anderson of Swansea: Up to two-thirds, I think.

Professor Sutton: Yes, indeed; that is clearly the major part. Where we are really working with colleagues in EDA is to look to areas where we can see this mutual benefit, again pointing to the capability need. But I would say that the contribution that other nations can make must come in two forms. Yes, we would like to see other nations frankly spending a commensurate percentage of their defence budgets on research and technology; but also our need to recognise that a good brain from Slovenia is as good as a good brain in the UK, and very often looking at some of the more fundamental areas of technology, even though it still has to align with capability needs, need not be horrendously expensive. But if we see that kind of a contribution, that kind of commitment then there are possibilities.

Chairman: I think that you have really discussed this question as to how the MOD would implement the Strategy in the UK. Could I turn to Lord Selkirk to ask his question, and could I apologise to him that it has been trespassed upon a certain amount by his colleagues.

Q68 Lord Selkirk of Douglas: Chairman, thank you very much. May I just preface my question by saying I think that you have in very large measure answered what I am about to ask, so if there is anything you would like to add to what you have already said that would be very welcome. Can I ask what progress has been made in mobilising the necessary capabilities, with particular reference to the transport helicopters for the EU's mission to Chad and to the Central African Republic? I think you also said in your comments that there was an insufficiency of helicopters. Could you summarise, in a few words, what you see as the solution to that problem?

Mr Mathewson: The EU has not yet identified the forces and capabilities that it needs for the Chad Mission. A series of options for this mission were identified and the PSC decided that the option that it would support was one that required around 4000 people. There have been three-force generation conferences so far, on 9, 14 and 21 November, and the forces have not yet been identified up to the level of 4000—I think we are some way short of it yet. Within that there are some critical shortfalls—a Role 2 hospital, fixed and rotary wing, both for tactical, logistics and medical purposes, and intelligence assets. At the moment the nominated Force Commander, the Operation Commander General Nash, is reporting to the PSC that he does not yet have the forces declared to him, identified to him that allow him to recommend to the PSC that the mission should be launched. So we are in a pause period where we have to reconsider the scale of the mission and whether the forces can be generated for the scale of the mission. At the moment no country has declared, I think, any helicopters at all, which I find surprising. So I think countries might be asked to reconsider whether it is genuinely the case that they cannot provide helicopters, and the EU may wish to consider some of the solutions which NATO has considered, for example contracting helicopter support for some of the very basic freight roles which is all that NATO is looking at. But I think it is surprising that none of the countries which are offering forces have offered helicopters.

Q69 Lord Selkirk of Douglas: I noticed in our briefing it is stated that Foreign Defence Ministers met in joint session to discuss the proposed ESDP mission to Chad. The Secretary of State for Defence underlined UK political support for the proposed mission as a key element in the comprehensive regional approach. Conclusions were agreed on current operations and missions under the European Security and Defence Policy, and he goes on to elaborate on that theme. Surely if they have agreed they should be able to put this altogether and get on with it?

Mr Mathewson: Yes. I think this is a gap between the political support for a mission and countries' willingness to declare forces. The position of the British government has been that from the outset they were clear with the EU that we would give

29 November 2007   Mr Andrew Mathewson, Professor Phil Sutton
and Captain Richard Stokes

political support but because of the strains on the forces in Iraq and Afghanistan we would not be able to provide forces for the mission. We are providing very small numbers of personnel to the operational headquarters, to the force headquarters, but we were not in a position because of current operational demands to provide any more significant contribution. I think this illustrates a problem for the European Union, that in theory there is a force catalogue which says that we can generate a force of 60,000, yet in practice we are struggling to generate a force of 4000. We can ask why that is. Is it significant that the United Kingdom is not participating in the force? I think it is disappointing if the EU cannot generate a force of 4000 without the United Kingdom; this ought to be within the range of ambition of other Members of the European Union. But I think there is this gap between what nations say they are politically prepared to do and their willingness then to provide the assets for it.
Chairman: Lord Crickhowell.

Q70 Lord Crickhowell: Can I move away from helicopters which we have covered pretty extensively this morning to a new element that you have just introduced, medical. Can you comment? All these operations will require medical supplies and medical facilities, and can you comment more about the European approach to this one and say more than you did in that rather throwaway remark that this was one of the problems in the Chad exercise?
Mr Mathewson: I do not know. I could certainly look at the data which we have in the force catalogue. The EU works on the basis that it asks nations to identify the forces they are in theory willing to commit to an operation, and there is this force catalogue that shows that the EU has sufficient forces in theory declared as potentially available to mount an operation of around 60,000, and that would include a full range of capabilities that a mission would require. I am certainly very happy to check.

Q71 Lord Crickhowell: Could we have a note perhaps on the medical point because it does seem to be a rather important one.
Mr Mathewson: Yes. I would expect that the force catalogue includes a number of countries that have declared hospitals in theory as available and they have not been offered on this occasion.
Chairman: Lord Anderson.
Lord Anderson of Swansea: Turning from Chad to Kosovo, clearly the EU would be playing a larger role there. Is there that same gap between aspiration and capability?
Chairman: Not militarily.
Lord Anderson of Swansea: No. Helicopters would be relevant, for example.

Chairman: With respect to Lord Anderson, the military operation in Kosovo is and will continue to be a NATO operation rather than an EU operation.

Q72 Lord Anderson of Swansea: But there will be a much grander EU operation on the civilian side and that will include, no doubt, relying on the military for the provision of helicopters and clearly across the board in that area, save for the NATO contribution from the military. What is the degree of preparedness of planning in response to a greater call for a civilian operation?
Mr Mathewson: I am afraid I simply do not know and the EU will, if the proper legal basis can be found, mount a policing mission in Kosovo to go alongside the NATO military mission, KFOR and replacing the United Nations in the policing role. The MOD is not actually very closely involved in planning the EU police mission and I have not so far been made aware of any concern about helicopters as being an issue in the EU policing.

Q73 Lord Anderson of Swansea: The police operation may require in an emergency rapid deployability.
Mr Mathewson: Yes, and clearly NATO has a rapid deployable capability for KFOR, but I am not sure that it has been raised as an issue in terms of the EU's police capability.
Chairman: Lord Hannay.

Q74 Lord Hannay of Chiswick: Following on this point about the difficulty of generating 4000 force for Chad and some specialist aspects to it, could you roughly rank in order of difficulty the problem that arises with regard to UN peacekeeping operations, the problem that arises with regard to NATO operations and the problems that arise in this case to the EU? Are they all much the same or are one of these three much better at generating forces when they take a political decision that they will become involved, because there is a really serious problem across the board, it seems to me, that one's method of approaching it would be different if it was merely identical in the case of all three organisations to which we belong or whether there were some which were better at it than others.
Mr Mathewson: I think as between the EU and NATO the issues are very similar, which is that nations declare what are on the face of it substantial forces, but those forces have not yet properly adapted to the requirements of deployable, sustainable expeditionary forces. NATO has issued planning guidance set out in its comprehensive political guidance about what sorts of forces it needs, emphasising the need to be able to deploy, sustain and reinforce on a deployed mission. Those are

essentially the same requirements as exist for an EU mission. So the challenge on the EU is essentially the same, albeit at a slightly lower scale and not across the full range of potential operations. I think what we are seeing in Kosovo and in Chad, part of it is aspects of a similar problem, that while nations have substantial Armed Forces they have not yet made the investment in the capabilities that make them deployable, whether that is deployable medical facilities, logistic support, the airlift. I think the scale of the problem is probably the same and the nature of the problem is probably the same for NATO and the EU. I think for the United Nations it is slightly different in that most of the logistics of what I think is provided essentially through UN arrangements, and they have their own logistic arrangements with which you, my Lord, will be more familiar than I am. There is less of a presumption in generating forces for UN peacekeeping that they are as fully deployable and fully as capable as they are for NATO and the EU operations.

Q75 *Lord Hannay of Chiswick:* Although from what the Under Secretary General for Peacekeeping is saying about the Darfur operation they are facing similar problems, although they are compounded by the unhelpfulness of the government of Sudan to allow certain units to be involved, but they do seem to be suffering from force generating capability problems too in that one. But I think there is a briefing by Lord Malloch-Brown and the Secretary of State for International Development this afternoon, so I will not waste more time at this meeting pursuing the matter here because I would like to raise it there.

Chairman: Thank you very much for having gone through the questions which we had let you have in advance. Can I thank you Mr Mathewson, Professor Sutton and Captain Stokes, we are really very grateful for you to coming to spend so much time with us and to enable us to really explore these things because it is, I think, probably only in this Committee that it is possible to go into some depth about our relations with the EU on defence matters—at least this end of the building—and we are therefore really grateful that you have found time to come to talk to us. I think you may be coming back with some of your DFID colleagues in the New Year to discuss some of the paper on fragile states and security, which was also discussed at the meeting on 19 November. Thank you very much for this morning's evidence.

Supplementary memorandum by the Ministry of Defence

The Committee requested further details on where those UK forces that will make up the Battlegroup have been deployed prior to the JRRF

1. The EU Battlegroup will be based on the Small Scale Focused Intervention (SSFI) Battlegroup. The SSFI will be found from two battalions:

— 2 RRF (2nd Battalion The Royal Regiment of Fusiliers) from 01 Jul to 01 Oct 08.

— 4 RIFLES (4th Battalion The Rifles) from 01 Oct to 31 Dec 08.

Until recently, 2 RRF were based in Cyprus and were the Theatre Reserve Battalion for Iraq and Afghanistan. In 2006 two Companies deployed for two months to Iraq, one Company deployed to Afghanistan for six months and the Battalion Headquarters and two Companies deployed to Iraq for four months. In 2007 there have been two four month deployments to Afghanistan, the first was split between two Companies and the second was for one company.

4 RIFLES are based in Bulford. Their most operational commitment was as a Battalion to Iraq from 01 Jun 07 to 01 Dec 07.

The Committee requested confirmation on how many days a Battlegroup should take to deploy and become operational

2. According to the EU Battlegroup Concept paper (5 October 2006), an EU Battlegroup is held at a readiness status of 5–10 days. This means that following the approval of a Crisis Management Concept (CMC) the Council has five days to decide whether to launch an operation; the Battlegroup must then start implementing the decision in the Joint Operations Area (JOA) within 10 days.

The Committee requested further information on the level of UK engagement in the EDA project teams and initiatives and how this compares to our European partners

3. The EDA Activity database currently contains 92 separate areas of activity including Integrated Development Teams, Project Teams, Projects and Programmes in the Capabilities and R&T directorates. Of these the UK is active in 31 areas. In comparison France and Italy are active in 60 areas, Sweden 42, Netherlands 41, Spain 39, and Germany 37. In addition we are taking a leading role in the Capability Development Plan and the Research and Technology Strategy.

4. The UK is also working with the EDA Armaments directorate in the area of Standardisation and UAV insertion into controlled airspace and with the Industry and Markets directorate in the area of European Bulletin Board, Code of Conduct on defence procurement, European Defence Technological and Industrial Base and rationalisation of the European Defence Technology and Evaluation Base.

The Committee requested details on the medical capabilities offered to the EU in the Headline Goal 2010 Force Catalogue

5. The medical capabilities offered to the EU in the Headline Goal 2010 Force Catalogue are summarised as follows:

Strategic medical evacuation:

— 3 strategic air transport aircraft (MEDEVAC);

— 1 ship hospital (Maritime Medical Treatment Facility Role 3[1]).

Tactical medical evacuation:

— 16 medium/heavy transport helicopters (MEDEVAC);

— 11 companies of ground-ambulances (MEDEVAC);

— 7 intra theatre airlift aircraft (MEDEVAC).

Integrated health and medical treatment:

— 11 companies providing medical logistics;

— 13 teams providing a medical treatment facility (role 1[2]);

— 8 teams providing medical Communication & Information Systems;

— 20 companies providing a medical treatment facility (role 2[3]: light manoeuvre);

— 8 companies providing a medical treatment facility (role 3);

— 20 companies providing a medical treatment facility (role 2 enhanced);

— 4 medical task force head-quarters;

— 10 companies providing a casualty staging unit (CSU).

The Committee requested details on Permanent Structured Cooperation in the area of the ESDP

6. The principle of "Permanent Structured Co-operation" was established with capability development in mind. It is designed to encourage the development of more effective military capabilities amongst EU Member States and is in line with UK objectives for improving the capabilities available for EU-led operations. It has always been part of our thinking that improved military capabilities developed by the 21 Member States that are also members of NATO will also be available to the Alliance.

7. To join Permanent Structured Co-operation Member States need to commit to fulfil the entry criteria in the Protocol. The criteria include committing to more intensive and substantive capability development, including through the EDA, and contributing to a Battlegroup. Permanent Structured Co-operation was designed to create political pressure for further capability development. This is consistent with UK objectives of getting other Member States to develop better capabilities, enabling them to shoulder more of the EU's burden in the areas of security and defence.

---

[1] Deployed secondary treatment facility, four surgical teams, 50–200 nursed beds.
[2] First stage of casualty treatment, usually integrated in a unit
[3] Facilities that receive or collect casualties from Role 1, refine treatment, resuscitate and priorities casualties for onward evacuation to Role 3 facilities.

8. To make Permanent Structured Co-operation easier to set up, easier for Member States to join and easier for Member States to be suspended from if they no longer meet the criteria, these decisions are taken under Qualified Majority Voting (QMV). All other decisions in the field of ESDP will still be taken by unanimity. Council will adopt a decision by QMV on:

—   Establishing Permanent Structured Co-operation and determining the list of participating Member States (QMV amongst the whole of the Council).

—   Confirming participation of a Member State that subsequently wishes to participate (QMV amongst those members of Council already participating in Permanent Structured Co-operation).

—   Suspending participation of a Member State should it no longer fulfil the criteria or its commitments (QMV amongst those members of Council already participating in Permanent Structured Co-operation).

The Committee asked us to confirm whether A400M had flown

9. We can confirm that the first A400M military aircraft is currently under construction and has not flown yet.

12 February 2008

Printed in the United Kingdom by The Stationery Office Limited
3/2008   392200   19585

ISBN 978-0-10-401241-3

9 780104 012413